Original title:
The Beauty of Winter's Silence Whispers of Frost

Copyright © 2024 Creative Arts Management OÜ
All rights reserved.

Author: Natalia Harrington
ISBN HARDBACK: 978-9916-94-554-4
ISBN PAPERBACK: 978-9916-94-555-1

Winter's Veil: A Canvas of White Dreams

Snowflakes tumble, a soft ballet,
Falling on rooftops, they dance and splay.
A snowman giggles with a carrot nose,
As squirrels skate by in their winter clothes.

The trees wear blankets, all fluffy and white,
While birds plan their schemes for a warm, sunny flight.
The chilly wind whispers silly little jokes,
As ice slips and slides beneath clumsy folks.

The Magic of Still Air Beneath the Ice

Icicles dangle like teeth in a grin,
While penguins strut past, inviting their kin.
The pond is a mirror, frozen and plain,
Where ducks quack in rhythm, what a silly refrain!

Old snowmen chat with a wink and a nod,
As snowball fights break out, the kids all applaud.
But watch out for flurries, they're sneaky and sly,
A snowball may land with a gleeful "Oh my!"

Secrets Told by the Dimmed Hearth

Crackling firelight whispers tales of the cold,
While hot cocoa steams with sweetness untold.
Marshmallows float like clouds in a cup,
As cozy socks huddle, never giving up.

Each log has a story, a chuckle or two,
Of elves playing tricks, making hot tea for you.
The glow from the hearth keeps the shadows at bay,
While we laugh at the frost biting red cheeks today.

Frosted Artistry in Nature's Slumber

Frozen landscapes look quite like a painting,
As reindeer tiptoe, their hooves gently fainting.
A snow angel giggles, arms thrown in delight,
With paw prints of rabbits, tiptoeing in white.

Crystal branches surely are nature's new jewelry,
As snowy owls hoot with an air of peculiar glee.
The world is a stage, where winter takes flight,
With snowflakes as dancers, enchanting the night.

Invisible Hand of Winter's Grip

Snowflakes dance upon my hat,
I swear they're plotting, just like a cat.
With every step, my boots make noise,
Echoing laughter that nature enjoys.

Frosty breath, I'm puffing like a train,
Why does winter bring such silly pain?
Slipping around like a clumsy deer,
Winter's grip has turned me to a sphere.

Enchanted Pines in a Shroud of White

Oh, the pines wear coats that shimmer bright,
But I bet they're cold, despite their height.
They sway and crack, like laughter in the breeze,
Plotting treetop antics with utmost ease.

Twinkling lights, though frozen in place,
Remind me of shapes that mock my face.
Each step I take, I wish for a train,
To whisk me away from this snowy strain.

Silhouettes of Serenity in Frigid Light

Shadows stretch like they just woke up,
Brrr, it's colder than an ice cream cup!
They shiver and giggle like schoolyard friends,
Counting all the ways that winter transcends.

With a snowman grin, they wink and slide,
Hoping to catch me, their stumbly ride.
But as I tumble and roll in delight,
I wonder if they'll join my slip and flight.

Glistening Idleness in the Chill of Night

The stars are frozen, or so it seems,
A chilly canvas for my wobbly dreams.
Moonlight giggles at my frosty sill,
As I tiptoe home, channeling my thrill.

Icicles hang like uninvited guests,
Quipping and jabbing, they put me to tests.
I marvel at their sharp, gleaming flair,
In a world where romance thinks it's unfair.

Stillness Beneath Icy Veils

Snowflakes dance like little flies,
In jackets puffy, oh my, oh my!
Squirrels in sweaters, looking so grand,
While penguins gossip, side by side they stand.

Chill in the air that wraps us tight,
Icicles forming, a dangerous sight!
Footprints in snow tell stories anew,
'Twas the dog, not me, who tripped on the goo!

Glistening Ghosts of the Night

Moonlight giggles, gives shadows a dance,
Snowmen sport hats—oh, what a chance!
Laughter echoes off frosty air,
While Santa stumbles, catching a scare.

Chili cooks bubble, the spice we can't find,
Hot chocolate spills—just my luck, never mind!
Polar bears waddle with fish on their toes,
While snowflakes wonder where the warm breeze goes.

Echoes of a Frostbitten Dawn

Sunrise peeks, but it's way too cold,
Noses turning red, a sight to behold!
The toaster's on strike, bread frozen in fright,
I slip on ice—what a comical sight!

Carrots for noses in snowman decor,
But wait, that's not the carrot, it's my old shoe's lore!
Teenagers bundled, with pouts on their face,
While puppies dart through with curious grace.

Frozen Echoes in the Air

Frosty whispers jiggle, like jellies on quakes,
While birds in mittens sing tunes of high stakes!
A snowball fight breaks out, oh what a scene,
As mom yells "don't throw!" from behind the evergreen!

Icicles dangle, like swords meant to drop,
But kids with sleds go zooming, then stop!
Snow angels giggle, wings outstretched wide,
Frosty tongues stick out, and then we all glide!

Tranquil Shadows on White Canvas

Snowflakes drift down, soft as a sneeze,
Making snowmen who shiver in the breeze.
A carrot for a nose, a button for an eye,
They look quite confused, oh my, oh my!

Winter's chill tells jokes with icy breath,
While penguins moonwalk, avoiding a mess.
Hot cocoa mugs giggle, steaming with cheer,
All while the squirrels practice ballet, oh dear!

Murmurs Beneath the Snow

Under blankets of snow, secrets do hide,
Gossiping snowflakes, with nowhere to glide.
The trees wear white hats, a fashion faux pas,
They shake with laughter—a snowball hurrah!

Frosty the snowman tells tales, oh so grand,
About snowball fights, and his time in a band.
But when winter sneezes, and the snow starts to melt,
He's got to be quick, or he'll just be a pelt!

A Dreamscape of Icy Stillness

Icicles dangle, resembling teeth,
Giggling softly, they hide underneath.
The blanket of snow, oh where did it go?
Underneath, little creatures throw a snowball show!

Chill winds whistle tunes of a frosty ballet,
While skaters glide by, dreaming all day.
But watch where you step on this slippery ground,
Or they'll have you dancing, with no feet around!

Ethereal Beauty of the Frozen World

Frozen ponds shimmer, like diamonds in sun,
But beware of the edges, they're not any fun.
Snowmen tell jokes, like a frosty comedian,
As puns tumble out, in a chilly median!

The hush of the snow, a joke on its own,
While foxes in scarves strut, feeling full-blown.
Winter's a giggle, wrapped up in a coat,
Laughing its way as we slip on the boat!

Icy Whispers Through Sleepy Hollows

In the chill, the trees do shake,
Squirrels slide on ice like cake.
Penguins strut in their best tuxedos,
While snowmen hold their frozen toes.

Snowflakes giggle, they drift and tease,
They slip on branches, fetch a breeze.
Frosted whispers tickle the air,
As rabbits hop, unaware of care.

Icicles hang like frozen spears,
Drawing laughs from passing deers.
The world is still with a snowy cheer,
As winter's pranksters draw near.

Twinkling Stars Above a Silent Plain

Stars winking down on a snow-white frame,
While shadows dance in the moonlight's game.
The owls hoot jokes, quite unimpressed,
As the cold makes the critters dressed.

Frosty bunnies with nose so bright,
Are hopping around with sheer delight.
Every flake tells a story or two,
Of snowball fights, just like a zoo.

Under the twinkle, mischief does creep,
Even the bears are trying to leap.
In this chilly world where giggles evoke,
Laughter erupts like a hot cocoa joke.

A Whispering Quilt of Snowflakes

A quilt of white on the ground so neat,
With snowflakes in rows, it's quite a treat.
They chatter and giggle, knitting their dreams,
As the sun peeks out, or so it seems.

Fuzzy mittens launched in the warm air,
Flapping like birds without any care.
Children slide down the slopes with a cheer,
While dogs frolic, wishing for a deer.

Snowmen grinning with top hats on tight,
Taking selfies in broad daylight.
Even the moon can't help but grin,
As winter's chuckles spiral and spin.

Winter's Embrace in a Silent Vigil

In this stillness, snowscape aglow,
The bunnies plot to overthrow.
With carrot-laden schemes up their sleeves,
They giggle softly, as mischief weaves.

Frosty trees with branches wide,
Waving hello to those who glide.
As squirrels host their snowy ball,
Chasing shadows that start to fall.

With giggles muffled in blankets of white,
Snowballs exchanged in the fading light.
Where laughter dances on icy air,
And chilly winds send cravings for flair.

Soft Glimmers Over Silent Valleys

Snowflakes waltz and swirl like cheese,
They dance with glee upon the breeze.
In coats of white, the squirrels drop naps,
While dreaming of the world in wrapped-up naps.

Trees wear coats, so fluffy and bright,
Yet penguins giggle, thinking it's light.
A bunny hops, his ears all a-flop,
As he searches for carrots—no luck at the shop.

The Lull of Snow-Draped Earth

Pillows of snow blanket the ground,
A place where the snowmen can all be found.
They argue about hats, and which one's the best,
While birds in their nests are taking a rest.

Icicles dangle like chandeliers grand,
But to melting sun, they can't make a stand.
A cat watches closely, paw raised to explore,
In hopes that the chilly won't chill her once more.

Frosty Horizons in the Stillness of Night

Stars twinkle brightly in the crisp sky,
While snowflakes giggle and float by.
A snowman with a carrot for a nose,
Wonders where the wolves go when it snows.

The stars might twinkle, just slightly askew,
Crystals of frost paint the night all anew.
But the chilly winds, with a sneaky little grin,
Sneeze on the snowmen, causing chaos within.

Celestial Chimes in a Frigid Landscape

In the frosty air, chimes ring so sweet,
While sleds race down in a giggly feat.
A dog barks loudly, lost in the play,
As kids hurl snowballs in a great fray.

Snowflakes chuckle, they float and then fall,
Creating a blanket, oh-so-soft for all.
Yet the cold wind whispers, with a playful tone,
'This winter wonderland is a chill-out zone!'

Elegance of a Quiet December

Snowmen grin with carrot noses,
While snowflakes jive in silent poses.
The ice skates squeak, a jazzy tune,
And hot cocoa waits, a warm cocoon.

Socks on cats cause quite a scene,
They chase their tails like they were in a dream.
Mittens dance upon the ground,
A winter ballet that knows no sound.

Frosty breath forms clouds in the air,
As laughter echoes everywhere.
Even the squirrels wear tiny hats,
Preparing for more than just their spats.

As twinkling lights begin to gleam,
We toast marshmallows and share a dream.
Chilly cheeks in a giggling spree,
Winter's punchline is pure glee.

Winter's Caress in a Whispering Wood

In the woods, the trees gently sway,
As snowflakes giggle and drift away.
Bears in pajamas take cozy naps,
While rabbits throw unplanned snowball scraps.

The moon snickers, casting a gleam,
On icicles that clutch at a beam.
A fox struts by, wearing a scarf,
Are those his moves, or just a laugh?

Elves are hiding, peeking out wide,
From tree trunks where they often reside.
A deer pirouettes, trying to glide,
In a waltz with snowflakes, giggling with pride.

Every whisper in the night air,
Transforms the cold into warmth and care.
Woolly hats bob and little boots slip,
As joy rolls around on a frosty trip.

Impressions of Silence on a Frozen Hearth

Crisp air crackles, a fresh new start,
While snowmen plot their winter art.
The fireplace snaps, a cozy roar,
As whispers of snow bring laughter galore.

Chairs waddle on legs made of ice,
While hot cocoa pours, oh so nice.
Frogs in tiny boots hop to find,
The punchline of winter that's one of a kind.

Blankets piled up, a mountain so high,
As kids play peek-a-boo, oh my!
Winter's jesters dance in delight,
In the glow of the hearth, warm and bright.

Crackling laughter fills the space,
In this playful, chilly embrace.
A sprinkle of joy, a dash of the bold,
As winter's tale of fun unfolds.

Snowflakes Dancing on the Breath of Time

Snowflakes twirl like tiny spies,
In a chilly world where laughter flies.
They tickle noses, what a sight,
As snowmen giggle late at night.

They dance with grace, no fear or care,
With frosty hats and icy hair.
Chasing squirrels that slip and slide,
In this snowy joy, we take great pride.

A snowball fight, a playful fling,
Each hit reminds us, life's a swing.
With cheeks so red and hearts so bright,
Who knew icicles could bring such delight?

So let's rejoice in this icy tale,
Where winter's laughs never seem to pale.
For in this frost, both wild and free,
We find the warmth of glee's decree.

A Silvery Breath in the Heart of Cold

A silver breath from frozen trees,
Tickles my toes with winter's tease.
The snowmen frown with carrot noses,
As snowball cannons form funny poses.

The chills are real, but laughter too,
As penguins waddle, just like you.
With frosty mugs and cozy cheer,
We sip hot cocoa and shed a tear.

The chilly air is crisp and bright,
Making us dance in snowy delight.
Each step we take, we glide and trip,
Like ice skaters on a comedy script.

With flurries swirling all around,
Every giggle is winter bound.
So bundle up, let laughter unfold,
In the silvery breath, we brave the cold.

Whispered Secrets in a Crystal Dream

Whispers float on frosty air,
Like snowy secrets hiding there.
With mittens on, we swap our tales,
Of snowball fights and slippery trails.

Noses bright, and eyes aglow,
We tumble down, a comic show.
With each soft thud, a joyful cheer,
As winter's secrets, we all hear.

Icicles hanging, a chandelier,
With frozen tales we hold so dear.
As marshmallow fluff fills our cups,
We share our dreams—huddle up, pups!

So when the world turns soft and white,
We find our joy in frosty flight.
With laughter shared and warm hearts beamed,
In whispered moments, we'll be redeemed.

Echoes of a Deep Freeze's Tender Touch

Echoes bounce on icy streets,
In winter blankets, laughter fleets.
When frosty friends all come alive,
With joyful antics, we all strive.

Snowball fights and frozen fun,
Ice skating races, all in one.
We glide and slip, we laugh and spin,
Who knew winter could make us grin?

Frosty footprints mark our way,
As chilly breezes start to play.
With plump snowflakes on our hats,
Are we wintry mice or chubby rats?

So gather round, let's warm this freeze,
In warm wool hats and fuzzy cheese.
With echoes ringing through the night,
We'll dance away till morning light.

Chill of the Quiet Moonlight

The moon hangs high, a silver pie,
Squirrels in pajamas dash by.
Penguins in boots strut with flair,
Snowmen grinning, without a care.

Icicles dangle like crystal swords,
Hot cocoa served with silly gourds.
Bunnies hop, wearing snowflake hats,
Even the trees are chuckling, like chatty cats.

The chilly breeze tickles my nose,
As snowflakes dance in fluffy rows.
Winter's a prankster, pulling a joke,
Every snowball's a launching poke.

Under the stars, we all share a laugh,
Snowball fights, the ultimate gaffe.
Nature's comedy show in full display,
As winter shimmies in its frosty ballet.

Frost-kissed Dreams Unfold

Morning arrives with a frosty cheer,
Hot cakes stack high, let's all draw near.
Pancakes? No, they're icebergs with syrup,
Winter breakfast, the frosty hiccup.

Dreams wrapped in layers, thick as a nail,
Waking up late, like a sleepy snail.
Sweaters that hug like a bear's big grin,
Holiday lights flickering, let the fun begin!

Snowflakes tickle the nose with delight,
Falling down softly, oh what a sight.
Sleds zoom by with squeals and yips,
Frost-kissed laughter, brightening trips.

The fireplace crackles, popcorn's popped,
Winter's magic never stops.
Sipping on cocoa, we giggle and grin,
In a world of frost, the fun begins.

Whispers in a Crystal Realm

In a kingdom where icicles rule,
Fairies skate on frozen pools.
Snowflakes gossip, swirling with glee,
They've got some tales, just wait and see!

Elves in socks that don't match at all,
Jingle bells ring, they have a ball.
Chilly critters dressed up like stars,
Marketing snowflakes, hiding under cars.

Frosty whispers travel far and wide,
The chilly breeze has nothing to hide.
Blinking lights giggle like little sprites,
While polar bears crash dance-offs at nights.

Under the moonlight, a tug-of-war,
With snowmen ready to settle the score.
In this crystal realm, so odd but bright,
Each laugh sparkles like diamonds in light.

Serenity Shrouded in Snow

Snow drifts lie like blankets of cream,
A soft hush falls like a soothing dream.
Robins wearing tiny mittens and caps,
Chirping their songs, giving snowdrifts slaps.

Beneath the frost, mischief does dwell,
A rabbit in slippers plotting to yell.
Nature giggles, a quiet little hoot,
As squirrels trip over their fuzzy-first boot.

Moonlit nights bring out the jest,
Where winter critters play freeze tag at best.
Huddled in mounds, the snowballs await,
That friendly face-off at half-past eight.

So raise a toast to nature's wise crack,
With winter's chill giving laughter a whack.
In frosted silence, the fun unrolls,
Like cartoons in snow, warming our souls.

Glacial Reverie

Chilly breezes tickle my nose,
Snowflakes dance in a comic pose.
I slip on ice with a clumsy flair,
As laughter echoes through the chilled air.

A snowman wearing a silly hat,
Stands guard near my neighbor's cat.
They share gossips on frosty nights,
About snowball fights and snowshoe heights.

Mittens mismatched, what a sight!
I wear one blue and one that's white.
Yet in this frosty, playful spree,
I'm just as happy as can be!

So raise a cup of cocoa near,
And toast to winter, full of cheer.
With giggles, blunders, and lots of fun,
This chilly season has just begun!

Frosted Whispers Among the Trees

Trees adorned in frosty lace,
Hide a squirrel's comical chase.
He leaps and slips, oh, what a show,
Singing 'I'm a winter pro!'

Icicles hang like pointy teeth,
While snowmen plot beyond belief.
With carrot noses, they conspire,
To start a snowball-tossing choir.

Snow angels giggle in the ground,
Each flap of wings creates a sound.
It's a wintery joke, oh can't you see?
Even the snowflakes join in glee!

As twilight falls, the moon peeks in,
A frosty grin begins to win.
Shadows chuckle in the night,
Whispers of jokes take flight!

Dances of the Northern Lights

Colors swirl in a playful dance,
While snowflakes join, given a chance.
They twirl around in the cold embrace,
Creating laughter in this serene space.

A polar bear's breakdancing skills,
Could give any dancer quite the chills.
He shimmies and slips on the icy ground,
Turning winter into a circus sound.

With every flicker and glow so bright,
Frosty friends come out at night.
They giggle and jive without a care,
In the glow of the frosty air.

So grab your woolly socks and hat,
Join the fun with your furry cat.
Together we'll dance in frosty cheer,
Till the dawn breaks crystal clear!

Celestial Compositions in White

Fluffy clouds are playing coy,
Cardinals flaunt their winter ploy.
With little chirps and snowy hops,
They fashion tunes that never stop.

Frosty windows are a canvas wide,
Where doodles seem to come alive.
A reindeer scribbles just for fun,
In cryptic rhymes, oh what a pun!

Glowing lights blink and cheerfully flash,
As snowflakes bounce with a joyful crash.
They twirl and swirl, oh what delight,
In this whimsical winter night!

So let the snowflakes fall in grace,
Creating smiles on every face.
In the chill of this frosty scene,
We find the warmth of laughter keen!

The Sound of Silence in Cold Reflection

Snowflakes dance like tiny stars,

while penguins try to win at golf.
They swing their clubs in icy bars,
 missing holes, and giggling, soft.

Shivering trees tell jokes so dry,

as icicles laugh and drop like flies.
A snowman sneezes; oh my, oh my!
At winter's humor, the world sighs.

Frosty breath escapes with a puff,

the wind chortles, chilly and bright.
Each snowball fight is just too tough;
 we're giggling tightly, pure delight.

Elves slip and slide on patches slick,

making snow angels in no time.
While reindeer dance their groovy trick,
 wearing mittens, they perfectly rhyme.

Cacophony of Stillness on Crystal Paths

Snow crunches beneath big boots,

as squirrels claim the snowflakes lose.
With snow pants on, they start to scoot,
while giggles echo, bright and loose.

Snowmen sing in cheesy tones,

carrots stuck for noses round.
While yetis wear those silly bones,
this cold turf's where joy is found.

Penguins prance like they own the streets,

in their tuxedos, oh what a sight!
Icicles jingle like chimes so sweet,
creating music through the night.

Winter's drama brings laughter grand,

as snowflakes fall and prance about.
With frosty fun, the world's so planned,
we dance with joy and sing out loud.

Ethereal Chill on a Starry Canvas

Stars twinkle like winking friends,

while snowmen sport some goofy hats.
With frosty noses, humor blends,
in snowball fights, they stop for chats.

Snowy owls wear quirky styles,

while children slide down hill with glee.
The essence of fun travels miles,
with laughter echoing joyfully.

Chickadees chirp in merry cheer,

hurling snowflakes, a silly game.
While frostbite threatens, never fear—
we chuckle loud; it's all the same.

Under stars, our mischief grows,

as ice castles glisten with flair.
With each chilly gust that blows,
dancing in winter's brisk air.

Serene Echoes Through Frosted Woods

Trees wear coats, all fluffy white,

as raccoons try balancing treats.
With winter's joy, they leap with might,
yet tumble down, oh what a feat!

Whispers of giggles fill the glades,

as snowflakes tickle noses bright.
Frosty wonders—just silly parades;
chasing shadows till the twilight.

Bunnies hop in a frosty daze,

wearing scarves that look quite bizarre.
In this quiet, the joy displays,
like twinkling lights on a Christmas car.

Amidst the chill, laughter comes alive,

as friends embrace the icy cheer.
Together we dance, hearts will thrive;
the winter's fun is truly near.

Frosty Mornings and Moonlit Shadows

When frost nips hard at my nose,
I dance around in my winter clothes.
Snowflakes swirl like a crazy waltz,
I trip and fall; ah, childhood vaults!

The moon grins wide, it sees my plight,
As I tumble under its soft light.
Chasing shadows that tease and flit,
I laugh so loud; my friend says, "Quit!"

Puppies too join this chilly spree,
Bounding around, as happy as can be.
Their frosty breath makes the night chuckle,
As they wrestle snowballs; oh, what a struggle!

So here's to mornings that spark delight,
Where winter's humor warms the night.
With each slip and slide, I find my cheer,
Frosty fun makes all woes disappear!

The Stillness of Snow-Covered Pines

Oh, the pines dressed in white, standing so tall,
They wear frosty hats, but can't see the fall.
I swear they gossip in whispers, so neat,
"Look at that fellow who slipped on his feet!"

The branches sway with a chuckle or two,
As I tumble through drifts, looking like a kangaroo.
Each flake a jester, nature's playful prank,
"Join us in silence!" they seem to thank.

Squirrels stick close, with cheeks full of snow,
They watch and giggle, "Hey, that's quite a show!"
With every landing, a poof of white dust,
I join in the laughter; it's all a must!

And as the evening wraps up the scene,
The stillness hums with a glow, so serene.
These frosty fellows bring laughter in line,
With snow-covered crowns, they truly shine!

Gentle Breath of a Frozen Dawn

At dawn when breath hangs like little puffs,
The world looks cozy, just a bit tough.
I step outside and hear a crackle,
Like popcorn ready for a cheerful tackle.

My fingers turn pink; oh, what a sight,
Trying to button up with all of my might.
The ground is slick, a treacherous affair,
I skitter and slide, but hey, who needs flair?

Birds chirp loudly, trying their best,
To break this cold spell; it's quite the jest.
"Why sing in the warmth when we freeze?" they say,
As ice-laden branches sway and sway!

But with each frozen breath comes a grin,
This chilly escapade whisks away sins.
So here's to the dawn with its frosty play,
Where laughter and frost fight for the day!

Silvered Landscapes and Glacial Hues

Oh, silvered scenes dressed in icy tones,
Where snowmen rise and reclaim their thrones.
I tried to build one, but it fell flat,
His carrot nose? A victim to a cat!

The hills are alive with sleds gone wrong,
As we tumble and giggle; wouldn't trade it for long.
Laughter rings out like sleigh bells at night,
With each roll and flip, what a wondrous sight!

Each frozen patch holds a secret delight,
A chance for mischief, to give us a fright.
I slip on a patch, a dance in the air,
"Look mom, I'm flying!" like I have no care!

So let this cold canvas become our stage,
Where laughter is bright, turning every page.
In silvered landscapes, joy finds its way,
As we stumble and chuckle at winter's ballet!

Twilight's Icy Serenade

The snowflakes dance and twirl around,
They pirouette without a sound,
A squirrel slips on ice with a squeak,
And winter's charm is truly unique.

The chilly breeze tickles your nose,
While frostbite jokes come in droves,
A warm hot cocoa hugs your hand,
As you trip on snow like it's unplanned.

Laughter rings through the frozen air,
As snowmen wear scarves with a flair,
Their carrot noses, slightly askew,
Laughing hard, they resemble you!

So grab your boots and join the fun,
Winter's antics have just begun,
From snowball fights to icy pranks,
Nature giggles while giving thanks!

Crystal Pearls on Velvet Ground

The world is wrapped in a sparkly sheet,
Like a fashion show for frosty feet,
Mittens wave to chilly hands,
As snowflakes giggle in frosty bands.

A frosty tree dressed in white,
Stands still, trying to take flight,
While flurries tease and hide away,
As if inviting you to play!

The frozen pond is a slippery zone,
Where skaters twirl like they're on loan,
A graceful leap turns into a slide,
Landing softly on winter's wide ride!

As laughter echoes in the cold,
Frosty tales of joy unfold,
Caught in snowdrifts, laughter loud,
In a winter wonderland so proud!

Secrets Held in Frozen Breath

With every breath, a puff of white,
Whirling secrets lost in flight,
Snowflakes whisper a frosty song,
A tale of winter that can't be wrong.

The icicles drip like frozen zest,
Nature's joke, a twisted jest,
Each slippery patch a hidden trap,
As we navigate by winter's map!

Children giggle, their cheeks like brats,
While making snow angels in suitable hats,
The shy snowman hides a silly face,
With eyes that gleam and a nose that's ace!

So gather round for winter's delight,
In this frosty, funny, snowy night,
With laughter echoing through the trees,
We find joy in winter's breezy freeze!

Twilight's Tender Embrace

The twilight sky, a canvas bright,
With snowflakes swirling, pure delight,
Snow whispers softly to the ground,
In its cozy arms, joy is found.

Parks are blanketed, magic near,
While children sled down without fear,
A tumble here, a flip or two,
With every crash, they laugh anew!

Fluffy critters in their winter wear,
Hiding from snowballs tossed with flair,
As hats fly off in the playful breeze,
Nature chuckles, "Just take it, please!"

So let this chill wrap you up tight,
In snow's sweet laughter, pure delight,
For winter's charm is goofy and grand,
A frosty hug from a playful hand!

Resplendent Stillness of the Night

Snowflakes dance like clumsy sprites,
Giggling as they tumble down.
Every flake a funny sight,
Leaving the trees with frosty crowns.

The moon chuckles in the sky,
Winks at the icy ground below.
Even the shadows ask why,
As hot cocoa claims the show.

Squirrels in scarves take a peek,
Wondering if they should stay.
"Are there any nuts to seek?"
In winter's freeze, it's quite the play.

Laughter lingers in the freeze,
As penguins try to make a snowman.
"Can we add a carrot piece?"
But the nose just keeps on ran.

Frosty Narratives in the Dark

Chilly tales the winter tells,
Of penguins slipping on their tails.
Snowflakes giggle, drop, and fall,
Like jesters at a frosty ball.

Icicles dangle from the eaves,
Like silly hats on winter's thieves.
Every flake a tale to spin,
Of the frost that makes us grin.

Cold winds whistle through the trees,
They sing of frozen buddy bees.
"Let's build a hive, oh what a blast!"
But all they do is shiver fast.

Toasty marshmallows, sweet delight,
Make cocoa warm on snowy nights.
Winter's laughter echoes wide,
As we bundle close inside.

Silent Snowfall Serenade

In blankets white, the world does sigh,
As snowflakes fall from a giggling sky.
Each delicate whisper makes us cheer,
"Hey look! A snowy chandelier!"

The trees wear coats of fluffy lace,
Complaining of the freezing space.
"I know we look like winter's props,
But do we have to wear the frosty tops?"

Snowmen wobble with goofy grins,
Made of snow, with coal for chins.
"Watch me do a frosty jig,"
They laugh and spin, it's quite the gig!

Icicles clink like chimes of glee,
In the frosted air, they dance so free.
Winter's humor fills the night,
As all things spark with frosty light.

Frosted Echoes of a Still Night

The whisper of frost has a punchline,
Making the moon giggle divine.
"Not another snowball fight!"
Echoes of laughter take flight.

Trees twinkle in their icy glow,
While raccoons rush on soft tiptoe.
"Are we a circus in disguise?"
As snowflakes fall from smiling skies.

Bunny hops with a twinkling nose,
"Watch me leap in frosty pose!"
Fluffy tails wag with delight,
Jumps and tumbles in the night.

Snowy whispers sneak around,
As hot cocoa warms the ground.
The fun of winter we embrace,
Frosty parties we all chase.

The Quiet Canvas of a Silvered World

Snowflakes dance like clumsy clowns,
Hats made of ice, and boots made of frowns.
Hot cocoa spills on a shivering paw,
Winter's embrace is more slapstick than law.

Frosted branches wave, a chilly cheer,
Whispering secrets that no one can hear.
Sleds zooming past, with laughter and screams,
In this white wonderland, anything seems.

A snowman's grin, it's crooked but bright,
Trying to throw snowballs with all of his might.
But the wind gives a nudge, and off he goes,
A whirlwind of giggles, as the frosty wind blows.

Winter wears a jester's cap, it's true,
Each chilly puff is a whimsy anew.
So let's embrace the chaos and play,
In this silvered world, we'll laugh all day.

Murmurs of Frost Beneath the Moon

Under the moon with a silly grin,
Snowmen debate who'll win in a spin.
One says, 'I'm handsome, a real frosty star!'
Another chimes in, 'At least I'm not a car!'

Icicles hang like teeth from a mouth,
While penguins slide north, trying to scout.
A snowball fight breaks, chaos in the air,
With goofy helmets, no one seems to care.

The stars laugh down on this giggly show,
As bunnies hop in their cozy winter glow.
Each frosty voice joins the joyful shouts,
Echoing whispers of fun all about.

And as the night wraps us snug like a quilt,
Laughter and snow, the perfect childhood built.
Beneath this moonlit patchwork delight,
Winter's embrace is a pure, silly sight.

Tranquil Reflections in a Shimmering Landscape

In a world draped with icing, so sweet,
Critters scoot by with fuzzy cold feet.
A squirrel slips, he's met with a thud,
Rolling in snow, making quite the big bud!

Frozen ponds are now stages for slides,
Where ducks wear tuxedos on slippery rides.
They quack in unison, a frosty debut,
While flapping their wings in a choreographed view.

A timid old snowflake begins the grand dance,
Spinning and twirling, he takes quite a chance.
He tripled and tumbled, fell flat on his back,
But laughter bursts forth, it's a wintery crack!

The reflections of giggles fill crisp, chilly air,
As frost-kissed moments float everywhere.
So let's sip our cocoa, embrace every blunder,
In this shimmering chill, we'll laugh and we'll wonder.

Silent Meadows, Frost-Kissed Dreams

In meadows where snowflakes blanket the ground,
A puppy in mittens prances around.
He leaps like a pogo, with all of his might,
Napping in snow, what a goofy sight!

Frost-kissed dreams play hide and seek,
With silly snow angels that wiggle and squeak.
Each plump little snowball is ready to fly,
But they mush in a hugs, oh my, oh my!

The trees gossip softly, their branches astir,
While icicles laugh as they joke and they slur.
Gliding through snow, who would've thought,
Winter's just nature's way of saying, "You're caught!"

So gather your friends for a frosty parade,
With big fluffy snowflakes, let's all make the grade.
In these silent meadows, let joy be the theme,
For winter's just playing, it's all a sweet dream.

Frosted Sighs Beneath the Stars

In the night, squirrels wear capes,
Chasing each other in ice mazed shapes.
Snowflakes twirl in a chilly dance,
While penguins plot their frosty romance.

Trees are dressed in a frosty gown,
While the groundhogs play peekaboo in the brown.
Every whisper comes with a giggle,
As the snowmen shake and start to wiggle.

Birds in coats sing off-key faint,
While icicles hang like a frozen saint.
The moon chuckles in gleaming light,
At silly snowball fights breaking the night.

With stars all around, the snowflakes gleam,
As winter makes the world a dream.
But underneath, there's laughter loud,
As creatures dance and get snowed in a crowd.

Moonlit Whispers in a Frozen Realm

Under the moon, snowmen make jokes,
As bunnies hop like silly folks.
Icicles drip like a cold faucet,
While bears daintily waltz around a closet.

A penguin slips on a flurry glint,
Making snow angels without a hint.
The night air filled with frosty cheer,
As snowflakes gossip while they appear.

Trees stretch their branches in a shiver,
While the hot chocolate makes everyone quiver.
Sipping cocoa, laughter rings loud,
In a world where winter wraps us in shroud.

Toasting marshmallows on a chilly stake,
The frost tickles, no one's awake.
As the moon beams laugh at our plight,
Winter glows with a chuckle tonight.

A Symphony of Quiet Beneath the Snow

Snowflakes waltz without a sound,
While critters skate all around.
Squirrels giggle in their coats,
As they waltz like fluffy little boats.

The night whispers with chilly air,
While rabbits sneak, unaware of a dare.
A seal flips over in a splash of fun,
As winter frolics till the day is done.

Quietly, the stars watch the scene,
While raccoons hunt for treats unseen.
An orchestra of crunch and laughter,
As snowflakes fall, they chase after.

Everyone bundled, their cheeks are red,
While snowmen await, but will not be fed.
A ballet of silence, but full of zest,
In the still of the night, they laugh with the best.

Icy Tendrils of Tender Silence

A frosty breeze twirls past my ear,
As polar bears dance without fear.
In their tuxedos, they slyly slide,
While winter giggles; what a ride!

The snow whispers secrets to the pine,
While frosty breath turns to a line.
Nothing quiet, all snowballs wait,
For someone to catch 'em, it's fate!

Kittens tumble in a snowy heap,
While owls laugh as they try to leap.
A tumble here, a skitter there,
Laughter echoes everywhere!

Beneath the stars, the world is bright,
With icy hugs that feel just right.
In the crisp of night, under the glow,
Winter dances, a frosty show!

Crystal Lullabies in the Air

Frosty flakes float down with flair,
Making snowmen, without a care.
They tip their hats, a chilly sight,
With carrot noses, pure delight.

Snowball fights on frosty grounds,
Laughter echoes, joyful sounds.
Slip and slide, oh what a fall,
Winter's giggles, we recall.

Icicles dangle, like frozen spears,
Beware your head, or shed some tears!
But when the sun begins to show,
Melted smiles arrive with glow.

Toasting marshmallows by the fire,
Hot cocoa dreams never tire.
In this cold, we warm our hearts,
With every joke, the fun imparts.

Hushed Meadows Beneath a White Veil

Fields of white, as soft as cream,
Where snowflakes dance, like in a dream.
But watch your step, oh what a slip,
Down I go, on ice, I trip!

Giddy kids in bundled gear,
Making angels, lots of cheer.
But one sly snowball flies with ease,
Lands on me, oh dear, oh please!

Bunnies hopping, oh so cute,
In fluffy coats, they trot and scoot.
But wait! A shadow zooms on by,
Just a squirrel in winter's tie!

Amidst the hush, a sneeze appears,
Echoed laughs ring in my ears.
Snowflakes giggle, all around,
In the quiet joy, we're spellbound.

Whispers of Ice in Twilight's Embrace

Evening falls, the stars ignite,
Frosty breath, what a sight!
Hot tea steaming, cozy and bright,
While snowmen plot their frosty fright.

Pet cats wear tiny winter gear,
They strut like kings, with no real fear.
Under the moon, they leap and prance,
Chasing shadows in a chilly dance.

Pine trees draped in fluffy white,
Swaying gently, what a sight.
But wait, what's that? A squirrel's play,
Hiding acorns, in dismay!

In this still, a giggle spills,
Tickling noses, warming chills.
With every crackle, joy can't hide,
In winter's arms, we laugh and glide.

A Tapestry of Quiet Dreams

Softly falling, crystals shine,
Nature's quilt, a perfect line.
Sleds and laughter fill the space,
With cheeks as rosy as a face.

Furry boots and woolly hats,
Racing down with joyful spats.
But lo! What's this? A slippery spot,
Down I go—snow's got me caught!

Whispers of the cold night air,
Make snowflakes dance without a care.
With dreams of warmth, and smiles awake,
In chilly bliss, no hearts can break.

Under stars, the world is still,
With hot cocoa, we sip and thrill.
In the hush, we find our cheer,
As winter's playfulness draws near.

Frosted Imprints on Slumbering Ground

In fluffy pillows, snow does lay,
A frosty bed for critters to play.
A squirrel slips, does a crazy dance,
But in slow-mo, looks like he's in a trance.

Snowflakes fall with a gentle grin,
They whisper secrets, but what's a win?
"We'll coat your car like a cold, white cake,
Good luck with that drive; it's all a fake!"

Hot cocoa spills in the snowy breeze,
As marshmallows float like cute little squeeze.
With every slip on the icy street,
I chuckle with glee, oh what a treat!

So here's to winter, the prankster of all,
Who turns us to kids with a slippery fall.
Let's frolic and laugh in this chilly spree,
Until shovels come out, oh woe is me!

The Shush of Snowfall on Ancient Trees

The trees wear blankets of soft, white fluff,
Covered in snow, looking all quite tough.
With branches drooping, they seem to tease,
"Catch my falling flakes, or try if you please!"

In the hush of night, they creak and sway,
Looking like giants in a game, they play.
"Look! I'm a snowman," I hear one say,
But who'll take 'em seriously after this fray?

Icicles hang like chandeliers bright,
Ready to drip on someone tonight.
"Oops!" one sighs, "Oops! Too much of me!"
As I dodge the downpour, how funny to be!

So here's to the trees in their white attire,
Holding secrets and snow, oh how they conspire!
With all their antics, I can't help but stare,
A wacky winter show—I'm glad I'm aware!

Crystalline Dreams Under the Frosted Sky

Stars twinkle gently in a blanket of white,
While snowmen gossip in the still of night.
"Did you see my carrot? It's quite a sight!"
"Hey, don't be jealous—mine's just right!"

The moon up high shares a knowing grin,
While reindeer laugh, let the games begin!
They prance and leap with a bounce and a twist,
Snowballs are flying; "What's this? I insist!"

With every crunch underfoot, oh what joy!
The pitter-patter of a playful toy.
"Tag, you're it!" says a squirrel from afar,
With frosty giggles—it's a winter bazaar!

Dreams of snowflakes drift like confetti,
A whimsical dance, keeping all ready.
In crystalline worlds, we can truly spark,
Laughter echoes through the frosty park!

An Arctic Serenade of Soft Indifference

The wind whistles tunes, all cheeky and bold,
While penguins gather, wearing their cold gold.
They flop and they slide, in the frosty glow,
"Is this a convention? Let everyone know!"

I trip on my boots, oh what a scene,
As a snowflake lands square on my green bean.
"Did you dress for winter?" my buddies all bow,
"Well, snow is just fluff; it'll melt anyhow!"

Polar bears chuckle at the rustling leaves,
"Why do you humans wear so many sleeves?"
They sip their hot tea, with a snowy grin,
While I slip and slide like I'm in a spin.

Embrace the chill, with laughter's sweet care,
For winter's just joking, with antics to share.
As long as there's fun in the frosty parade,
We'll dance with the chill, it's a whimsical trade!

Clarity in Cold: A Wistful Reflection

Snowflakes dancing with glee,
Piles of fluff, just wait and see.
Sleds and laughter fill the air,
Look out! Here comes my flying hair!

The frosty breath of winter sighs,
Chasing rabbits, oh what a surprise!
With mittens lost and toes so numb,
Who knew snow could make me so dumb?

Icicles hang like boomerangs,
Each one a shield of chilly clangs.
Hot cocoa spills all down my pants,
Looks like winter is my clumsy dance!

Under layers, I waddle and sway,
Winter fashion, or so they say!
With snowmen made of snacks and fluff,
Who needs summer? Winter's just enough!

Shimmering Serenity in the Night's Grasp

Stars above in a frosty haze,
Dancing shadows in icy displays.
Why did I step out in flip-flops?
Now I'm hopping like a bunny who plops!

Chattering teeth are on display,
While the moon jokes, 'Stay in, okay?'
Winter's sparkle, a comical sight,
I trip on snow and giggle at night.

Carrots adorn a jolly snow face,
Why is he grinning? Just a mix-up in place!
Ice slides may seem like a fun game,
Until your backside's a part of the frame!

Chilling winds whip through my hair,
A nice look, if you're into despair!
Yet with a laugh and a little cheer,
Winter's humor brings us near!

Moonlit Paths Wrapped in Frozen Grace

Footsteps crunching on a white sheet,
Too careful to dance on frosty feet.
I slip and slide—but what a show,
Maybe next time I'll stick to my toes!

The moon winks down, teasing my plight,
Trying hard not to laugh at my fright.
Snowball fights turn into snowball fairs,
Socks as mittens? Fashion beyond compare!

Pine trees draped in shimmering white,
They whisper secrets of frosty delight.
But my nose is red; I look like a brat,
Maybe winter's just a big fluffy cat!

Each flake that falls is a tiny jest,
Snowflakes are here, put to the test.
While winter twirls and sways with grace,
I'm just trying to keep up in this race!

Tranquility in an Icy Mirror

A frozen pond, a mirror so clear,
Why do I feel like a cartoon deer?
Skating on ice, a graceful ballet,
Except I'm flailing, like a fish out of play!

With snowmen built to look like the dad,
I swear he's judging; it's making me mad!
He can't throw snow, but I bet he'd try,
If he had hands, surely he'd comply!

Hot soup in a bowl, my perfect delight,
But winter says, 'Chill, take a bite!'
Slippery steps, a comedic show,
Winter's antics make me glow!

The icicles wink as they dangle with grace,
While flickering flames offer warmth in this space.
Oh winter come, let's laugh and play,
For even cold days can warm hearts in sway!

Milton Keynes UK
Ingram Content Group UK Ltd.
UKHW022011131124
451149UK00013B/1110

9 789916 945551